Another Annie Mouse Adventure
Sixth in the Adventures of Annie Mouse series

Annie Mouse's Second Route 66 Photo Journal

The Journey East

Written by **Anne Maro Slanina, Ph.D.**
Illustrated by **Melinda Hood**

I was so excited! We were finally on our way to another Route 66 adventure AND this was my first airplane ride!

Our last Route 66 trip ended in Needles, CA with our visit to Cousins Mary and Bob. Mommy and Daddy had promised them we would be back for another visit. We had such a great time that we'd been planning another Route 66 family vacation ever since! Route 66 goes from Chicago, Illinois to the Santa Monica pier in California and we wanted to complete the entire route.

We were flying to California because Daddy said we would have enough time to visit relatives and complete the entire route if we flew to Los Angeles, then drove the route from west to east. I couldn't wait for the school year to end and our trip to begin!

Before we left for the trip we had a wonderful surprise! Cousins Mary and Bob's daughter, Penny, called and said that she was going to be moving from Los Angeles to Chicago and would enjoy our company for the long drive east. She loved Route 66 and was eager to share the trip with us. She picked us up at the airport.

As soon as I saw her van, I knew this trip was going to be fun!

As Penny raced through traffic, I closed my eyes and Daddy said he was thankful that he didn't have to do the driving! Mommy said she'd never seen so many cars on one road before! Penny wasted no time getting us to our first stop, the Santa Monica pier and the end of Route 66.

Penny said we had to mark an official start to the trip with a picture around the shop with the "End of the Trail" sign: 66 to Cali.

Starting the Journey East

We had a fun day enjoying all the activities at the pier. We rode the Ferris Wheel, swam in the Pacific Ocean and played on the beach.

While Daddy took my older brothers to the shooting gallery, Mommy and Penny took the rest of us to the aquarium. We agreed to meet at the end of the pier by the tribute to Bob Waldmire wall. We learned about the famous Route 66 artist on our last trip. We went inside the shop and each of us picked out a post card with his art work as a souvenir.

A Tribute Wall to Bob Waldmire

The Santa Monica pier arch looked really cool all lit up at night!

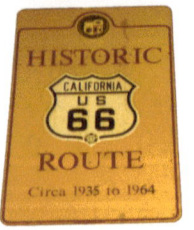
After leaving the Santa Monica pier, Penny drove down Santa Monica Blvd. She took us to a really cool diner in West Los Angeles, the Café 50's. The adults played trivia games. Even I knew the answer to where Route 66 begins! Us kids colored pictures while we waited for our food. Penny told the waitress she was a big kid and wanted a picture to color, too! The waitress hung our pictures on the wall when we finished them! The best part was that Daddy said we could all have a milkshake, too!

Our first stop the next morning was the Hollywood Walk of Fame. We had fun reading the names on the stars. This was my favorite one!

It was getting so crowded along the walk that I was getting scrunched! I made sure to stay close to Mommy and Daddy so I wouldn't get lost like I did on our last trip, but it was getting harder and harder to keep all of us kids together! That's when Penny suggested we take a guided tour on a bus. She said we'd be able to see a lot more without having to walk in the crowds or drive in the traffic.

↖ Grauman's Chinese Theatre ↗

Everyone loved the bus tour! We got to see where all the famous television and movie stars lived, the famous Hollywood sign, Beverly Hills and Rodeo Drive, where Penny said all the super-rich people shopped. Best of all, our bus ticket included admission to the wax museum. The wax figures were of all kinds of famous people, even presidents, movie and TV stars, athletes, and musicians. They all looked real! We were allowed to walk right into the displays and pretend we were a part of the sets. We had a lot of fun!

After a fun, but exhausting day, Penny finally stopped in Pasadena for the night.

Early the next morning we all piled back into Penny's van and continued our journey east, taking the old Foothills Blvd. alignment of Route 66. Brother Bobby pointed out the unusual-looking Aztec Hotel in Monrovia. Penny said that even though it was called Aztec, it is Mayan architecture and was built in the 1920s.

Big Sister Jenny wondered if we could see a movie at the Azusa Foothill Drive In Theatre, but Penny told us it closed a long time ago and the only thing left of it is the sign. Mommy thought the San Gabriel Mountains behind the theatre looked like a painting.

Big Brother Sam was the first to see the Madonna of the Trails statue in Upland. On our last trip we saw a similar statue in Albuquerque and learned that twelve of them had been placed along the Old National Trail to honor the role pioneer women played in the country's westward expansion.

Penny slowed the van down as much as she could for me to take this photo of the overpass that announces "America's Main Street Route 66" along with the shapes of each of the eight Route 66 states. Pretty cool, huh?!

A statue to honor the women who helped settle the west.

Route 66 America's Mainstreet

Bono's Historic Orange in Fontana was closed, but Penny told us it used to sell orange juice from this orange-shaped road stand. The sign said it would be reopening soon.

We all got excited when we saw the Wig Wam Motel in Rialto come into view. I wanted to stay in a Wig Wam! We were disappointed to learn that they were all filled for the night. Mommy said we'd make reservations next time. How exciting! Mommy is already thinking about another trip!

I'm looking forward to staying in a Wig Wam next time.

In San Bernardino this car advertised Juan Pollo's chicken.

We learned that the very first McDonald's restaurant started in San Bernardino and the site is now a museum. The murals on the outside of the building were amazing! Daddy liked the old signs from Route 66 inside the museum. I liked looking at all the toys. It was hard to keep Billy and Buster from trying to play with them!

11

Our next stop was in Victorville. This old truck marked the site of the California Route 66 Museum.

As Penny continued driving through the desert, we approached what looked like a wall of colorful bottles! Penny told us this was Elmer Long's Bottle Tree Ranch, and the bottles were sculptures. We were allowed to get out and walk through the display. We had never seen artwork like this! Some of the colored bottles clinked together gently in the breeze and made such a pretty sound.

Back in the van, it seemed like a very long time until we finally stopped in Barstow.

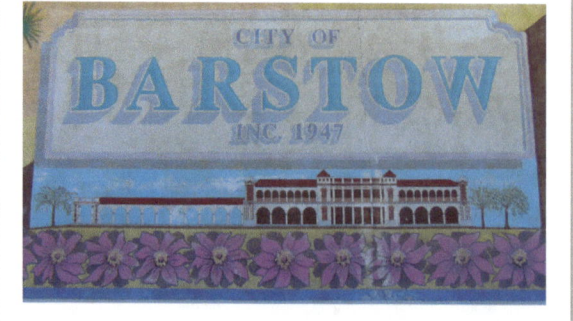

Big Brother Bobby was the first to see this house with an unusual roof in Daggett. Penny told us it's known as the ski lodge roof house and was once a café.

We were all ready for some nice, cold drinks! Penny stopped at the Bagdad Café in Newberry Springs. She told us it was famous because it was the set for a movie of the same name a long time ago.

We discovered that there was once volcanic activity in the Mojave Desert as we drove past the Pisgah Crater lava field.

We stopped for lunch at the Ludlow Café and learned that Ludlow used to be a mining town. At first I was afraid to go inside because I saw the word "dynamite" on the mining car, but Daddy explained that it was just a display to show what they used for mining here in the 1880s.

This sign at Roy's Café was my favorite thing in Amboy.

As Penny continued driving, we noticed the rocks along the sides of the road were spelling out names. Sam asked Penny if we could get out and all write our own names, but Mommy said, "NO!" So instead, we started a contest to see who could read the most names.

↖ Someone wrote Emilio! ↗

Penny told us to watch for the "Guardians of Route 66," which are two lion-like mysterious statues. "No one seems to know what they are or how they got there," she said. Bobby was the first to see them, shouting, "There they are! Can we get out to see them?" Before getting out, Penny warned us to watch out for snakes. Bobby found a journal behind the statue and we all wrote our names in it before getting back in the van.

We were finally going to see Cousins Mary and Bob! Penny was excited to be seeing her parents, so we were all surprised when she pulled the van into Fenders River Resort instead of going to their house. It didn't take long to figure out why! As soon as we got out of the van, Mary and Bob came running towards us.

We were going to have a family reunion at Fenders for a few days! Mommy and Daddy couldn't believe Penny kept this a secret from us! Penny couldn't stop giggling. Even Rosie, the manager of Fenders, was in on the surprise. I was excited to discover that we were going to camp there for a few days. We had a blast! We went tubing in the Colorado River, swam and had a picnic.

The next day we had a chance to explore more of Needles than we did the last time we were here.

Office building of Michael P. Burger, CPA. Used with permission.

We visited the Conestoga Wagon and ate at one of our favorite restaurants from the last trip, The Wagon Wheel, which had some cool murals painted on the sides.

Before leaving Needles, Cousin Mary said she hoped I was making another photo journal of this trip. "Of course," I said, as I held up my camera to show her.

There were lots of hugs as we said good-bye to Cousins Mary and Bob, and our new friend, Rosie, and then we were on our way to Arizona. As Penny drove away Daddy said we should have a family reunion at Fenders every year. I hope we do!

As we crossed the Colorado River into Topock, Arizona, Penny slowed down so I could get a picture of the Old Trails Arch Bridge. It was once used for cars to cross between California and Arizona, but now it supports an oil pipeline.

As soon as we saw burros on the street we knew we were entering Oatman, the old gold mining town that still looks like an old Wild West town. We were just in time to see the Wild West street show.

The burros were originally used by the miners to help carry gold ore and mining equipment. Now they roam the streets looking for carrots from tourists and try to get into the shops! Penny warned that not all of them were friendly and, since they are wild animals, we should be careful.

As we walked past the mine entrance Sam read the warning that we should never enter an abandoned mine, but this one was for tourists to explore.

After leaving Oatman, Penny expertly guided the van through the windy, narrow Back Country Byway, passing through Sitgreaves Pass.

In Penny's van, we were much higher up than when we were in our car and I was able to see so much more! The view was amazing, but a little scary! Penny warned us that at some points it might look like we could fall off the road, but we shouldn't worry because she had driven this route many times before and would keep us safe.

Penny couldn't get gas at Cool Springs since the pumps were just a display, but we all filled up on nice cold bottles of Route 66 soda!

On our way to Kingman we passed the ruins of Ed's Camp.

Sam wondered how they got the horse and wagon to stay on top of Mike's Outpost!

In Kingman we visited the Mohave Museum of History and Arts. On our way inside we examined the mural, which told the history of Kingman through its pictures.

There was a lot to see and do in Kingman, but my favorite thing was climbing on the steam engine in Locomotive Park!

We enjoyed burgers and ice cream at Mr. D'z Route 66 Diner, then drove around to see the neon signs lit up.

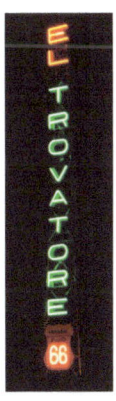

At Route 66 Antares Point Visitors Center we met the artist, Gregg Arnold, who created the giant, green head sculpture that greets visitors. He told us it was 14 feet tall and he had named it Giganticus Headicus. We walked around the building admiring more of his artwork, before going inside and getting snacks and souvenirs

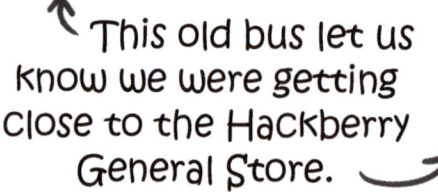

↑ This old bus let us know we were getting close to the Hackberry General Store. →

There was a lot to explore at Hackberry General Store! Every corner, and even the restrooms, had something interesting to look at! Penny bought a tee-shirt and Daddy bought a few more Route 66 books.

With this huge sign, Penny couldn't miss the entrance for the Grand Canyon Caverns!

We had a great time exploring the animal rescue, Keepers of the Wild, in Valentine.

Penny was so excited about stopping at the Grand Canyon Caverns that she finally told us she had a surprise. We were going to meet a special friend of hers, Mr. Jim Hinckley, a Route 66 author. He was here doing a book signing. Mommy and Daddy had purchased several of his books on our last trip and we had been using them to plan this trip. I couldn't believe we were going to get a chance to meet him! We bought a copy of his latest book and he even autographed it for us!

We had another surprise: Daddy bought tickets for the cave tour! We learned that this is the largest dry cavern in the United States; there is no natural light inside, and no animals or bugs can live inside.

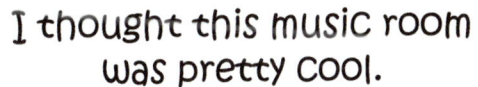

Our tour guide showed us a special room that people could stay in overnight!

I thought this music room was pretty cool.

We were allowed to play outside for a little while before getting back in the van. There were giant dinosaurs that were so cool!

Our next stop was Seligman. Penny told us that it was one of the most important towns on all of Route 66!

We stayed a few days in Seligman, which is known as the birthplace of historic Route 66. After I-40 bypassed the town it was in danger of becoming a ghost town. The barber, Angel Delgadillo, worked to get the state of Arizona to declare Route 66 a historic highway and tourists began coming back to Seligman. Angel's barber shop now includes a visitor's center and gift shop.

We shopped at the General Store and explored the display of Old West buildings that we learned is often used as a movie set.

We were allowed to sign our name on this van parked outside the Route 66 Motoporium. When we went inside we discovered it was a gift shop and also a museum with motorcycles, old cars and lots of antiques.

We ate a yummy breakfast ← at the Road Kill Café.

Our lunch at Delgadillo's Snow Cap Drive-In, was served with lots of jokes, starting with two knobs on the entrance door! We all laughed when Penny couldn't open the door! Can you guess why she chose the wrong knob?

We had dinner and delicious pie at Westside Lilo's. The hanging bottles on the side of the building reminded us of Elmer's Bottle Tree ranch in California.

As we headed out of Seligman, we saw this really cool sign.

 As we entered Ash Fork this sign welcomed us to the "Flagstone Capital." Daddy explained that the walkway that goes from our house to the driveway is made from flagstones. We spent a lot of time in the Ash Fork Route 66 Museum, exploring the displays and artifacts from days gone by.

 Next, we stopped in Williams, which is known as "The Gateway to the Grand Canyon." On our last trip, we took the Grand Canyon Railroad tour. That was a lot of fun, but this time we decided to experience the drive-through wildlife park, Bearizona.

After walking up one side and down the other of Route 66 in Williams, we finally took a break!

 As we continued the drive east we noticed that things began to look a lot greener. The pine trees reminded me of our yard in Pennsylvania. Penny said Parks in the Pines General Store had great sandwiches, so we stopped there for lunch and ate outside at the picnic tables.

Our first stop in Flagstaff was at the Visitors Center, where they helped us plan our day. We saw Riordan Mansion State Historic Park and the Lowell Observatory. We strolled through the downtown historic district. We cruised Route 66 and stopped for ice cream sundaes at Miz Zips!

Isn't this a cool sign for The Museum Club?

This was my favorite neon sign in Flagstaff.

We were excited to see the two big arrows were still standing at Twin Arrows, but we were sad to see all the graffiti on the diner and trading post.

Mommy and Daddy wouldn't let us get out of the van and explore at Two Guns. Instead, Penny drove through the ruins of what used to be a roadside attraction.

We stopped to take pictures at the Standin' on the Corner Park In Winslow, and discovered two statues: the original and a new bronze statue of Glenn Frey, who co-wrote the song that helped make Winslow famous.

← Daddy took us to the Old Trails Museum while Mommy and Penny went shopping. →

We enjoyed the art gallery and gardens at La Posada Hotel. It cost more than a million dollars to build in 1929 and was known as one of the fanciest hotels on Route 66! Mommy and Daddy reminded us not to touch anything while we were inside!

We discovered this mosaic of a jack rabbit in the sidewalk as we entered the Jack Rabbit Trading Post, Penny bought a tee shirt that looked just like the Jack Rabbit's HERE IT IS sign to add to her collection.

At the Geronimo Trading Post we saw the world's largest petrified tree!

↑ Penny took a family photo for us at the Jack Rabbit Trading Post. I think this might be the largest rabbit I've ever seen.

We had a delicious Mexican dinner at Joe & Aggie's Café and slept in a wigwam!

Stewart's Petrified Wood was a great place to explore! Not only did they have lots of dinosaur statues, they had real, live ostriches, too!

We stopped at the Painted Desert Indian Trading Center to visit with the friends we'd made on our last trip. We wanted to play on the big dinosaur in the yard, but Mommy told us all to notice that the sign says to stay off! Inside, we visited with our friends and Daddy let us each choose a small bag of colorful rocks from the bins.

Our last stop in Arizona was at Chee's Indian Store where Penny got excited about finding an autographed book she'd been looking for.

On the way out of Arizona we drove past the shops and admired the carvings on the side of the mountain.

As we crossed the state line into New Mexico, I stared out the window at the beautiful rock formations. Before I knew it, Penny arrived in Gallup. A train coming down the tracks as we approached downtown reminded us that Gallup began as a railroad town.

Check out the cool sign that directed Penny where to park! At the Rex Historical Museum, we learned about Native American culture and the history of the railroad and mining in Gallup. Many talented Native American artists live in Gallup, which is why it's known as the Indian Jewelry Capital of the World.

Penny liked this horse, which was created using the horse hair pottery technique, so Daddy bought it for her, to thank her for being such a great tour guide! It even has a turquoise stone for an eye!

I spotted this statue, known as a "Muffler Man," standing on top of a building.

There were many colorful signs in Gallup. Here are a few of my favorites.

28

We stayed at the El Rancho Motel, the "home to the movie stars." Many western movies were once filmed in the area and many of the stars stayed here. Each door has the name of one of those stars. Mommy and Daddy requested the Jimmy Stewart room, who starred in the movie, *It's a Wonderful Life*. We watched the movie and visited the Jimmy Stewart museum in his hometown of Indiana, Pennsylvania, during our winter break from school.

The Continental Divide marks the point at which rain water flows either to the east to the Atlantic or to the west to the Pacific Ocean. We stopped to buy snacks and look inside the hogan, a traditional Navajo dwelling.

Penny said Grants was a "must stop" because it was filled with many of the old "Googie-style" signs. These were my favorites.

Sally spotted a park and asked if we could get out and play for a little while. As Penny parked the van, she pointed to the top of the beautiful metal sculpture bordering the park and told us the symbol is called a Zia. It's the same symbol that looks like a sun on the flag of New Mexico.

In San Fidel I spotted this pretty church, but Bobby was the first to spot the Zia symbol on this sign.

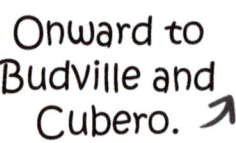

Onward to Budville and Cubero. ↗

We passed by the trading posts in Cubero and Budville as Penny made her way to New Laguna.

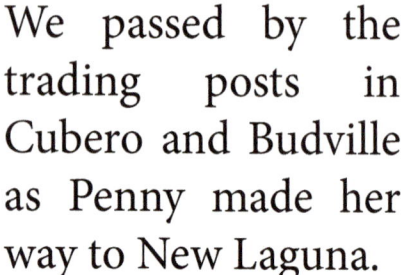 We shared huge, delicious burgers at Laguna Burger, the 66 Pit Stop.

The Rio Puerco bridge was built in 1933 and is now closed to traffic, but we were allowed to walk across it! A sign told us that it was built in 1933 and at 250 feet in length it is one of the longest in New Mexico.

In Old Town Albuquerque we shopped and visited the Sculpture Garden at the Albuquerque Museum.

We took a break at the 66 Diner. Over milkshakes, Penny pulled out her map to discuss the next part of the trip. At different times in history, Route 66 took different paths. After learning what everyone wanted to see, she agreed to drive a section of what is known as the Santa Fe loop, which was an original Route 66 alignment, then go back to Albuquerque and drive the newer alignment so we wouldn't miss anything. When we were done with our milkshakes, we took a family photo by the "Pile-Up Wall."

We ended the day at Sandia Peak Inn. As she admired the beautiful sculptures in the middle of the parking lot, Mommy said it seemed like we were at another art museum!

The next day, Penny took the pre-1937, Santa Fe route, and didn't stop until we arrived at Pecos National Historical Park. My favorite part was exploring the ruins of the Pecos Pueblo and Spanish Mission church. I was glad we didn't see any snakes!

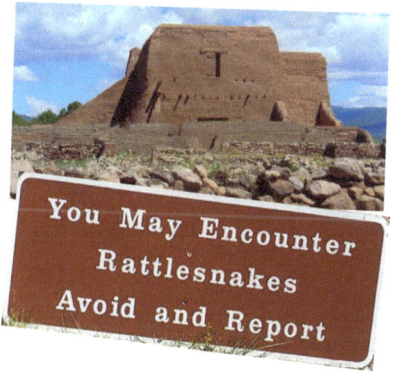

After leaving Pecos National Historical Park, Penny drove back the way we came so we could spend the next day in Santa Fe before going back to Albuquerque.

There were so many interesting things to see in Santa Fe, which is the oldest city in New Mexico. As we walked through the historic district, we stopped in museums and shops. We visited San Miguel Church, the oldest church structure in the U.S., built around 1610. We toured Loretto Chapel, where we saw what is called the "miraculous staircase" because of the way in which it was built.

↑ We also ↑ visited the Oldest House in the USA, which was built around 1646.

Back in Albuquerque we had hot dogs at the Dog House and stayed in vintage trailers at Enchanted Trails RV Park & Trading Post. →

As Penny continued the drive east she came to the section of the road known as the Music Highway. We had to be very quiet in order to hear the song, America the Beautiful, coming from the road. It was so cool, Penny turned around and did it all over again!

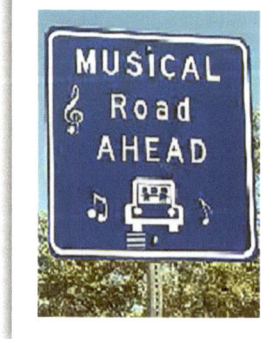  

These horses welcomed us to Moriarty. On our way to the toy museum, we all recognized the colorful, Googie-style, star above the restaurant sign.

CLINES CORNERS

Penny stopped for gas at Clines Corners. Mommy insisted we all take a restroom break before joining Daddy at the snack counter. When Penny joined us inside, she went right for the tee-shirt rack! I wonder where she's putting all of them!

When we got to Santa Rosa, Penny had a great idea: a picnic at the Blue Hole! Penny ordered a variety of her favorite Mexican food items "to go" from both Joseph's and Silver Moon. When we arrived at the Blue Hole, Billy asked if we could go swimming, but Daddy reminded us that the water is too cold; people come here to scuba dive and they must wear special suits. We set out our picnic blanket and assortment of food and watched the scuba divers while we ate.

As Penny drove through Santa Rosa, we looked for interesting signs. Penny's favorite was the Club Café. I spotted another Zia and Sam noticed the Googie-style sign right beside it! Daddy's favorite was from the auto museum.

33

 Penny said Cuervo was her favorite ghost town on the route. We could see the town's name written on the side of the mountain. Everything looked frozen in time and I wondered where all the people went.

This sculpture welcomed us to Tucumcari. There was so much to see and do; we stayed for a few days!

We discovered Timeless Treasures was now called "Tucumcari Trading Post." Penny explained businesses on the route often change, so the trip is never the same twice. Mommy and Penny went inside while Daddy and the rest of us looked at all the antiques outside. They came out with lots of packages, so it must still be a great place to shop!

 They came out with lots of bags from Tee-Pee Curios and The Trade Station, too! Penny bought MORE tee-shirts!

We went to several museums.

The Gallery, Art Museum

Mesalands Dinosaur Museum & Natural Sciences Lab

Tucumcari Historical Museum

We enjoyed delicious food and treats in Tucumcari.

There were so many great motel choices, Daddy said we'll just have to keep coming back until we could stay in them all!

Our last stop in New Mexico was at Russell's Truck & Travel Center. It was much more than a gas stop! Daddy and my older brothers went straight to the car museum, but Penny stopped in the gift shop to look at all the tee-shirts! It even had a huge café inside!

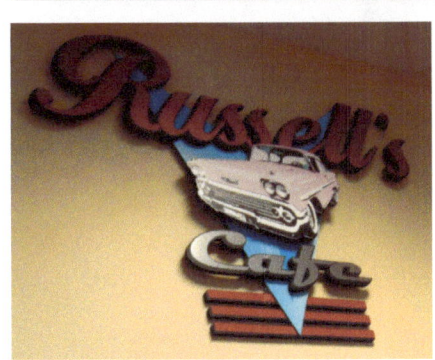 

When we crossed the state line into Texas, the remains of the "First/Last Motel in Texas" and a closed gas station reminded us that Glenrio was once a popular stop for travelers.

We all cheered when we arrived in Adrian - the official halfway point of the route. At the Midpoint Café, Mommy, Daddy, and Penny ordered several different kinds of their famous "ugly pies" for all of us to share. My favorite was the apple.

Next door to the Midpoint Café, at the Sunflower Station I got to sign my name on the truck parked beside the building!

Next stop, Vega!

In Vega we stopped at the Visitors Center in a restored Magnolia Station. We also explored all the treasures at Dot's Mini Museum and were excited to see the boot tree was still there!

Even though we'd been to the art display called Cadillac Ranch on our last trip, we all wanted to spray paint our names on the cars that were planted in a row in the ground.

Our next stop was the Historic 6th Street area in Amarillo. Penny parked the van near the 6th Street Antique Mall and we explored the various shops. Inside the antique mall, Mommy was happy to find a pitcher exactly like one she'd broken that had been her grandmother's. We each picked out a special Route 66 Christmas tree ornament at Amarillo's

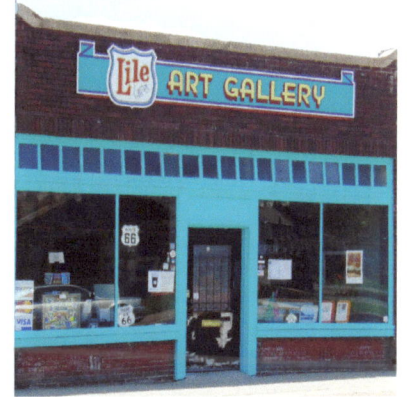

Route 66 store. I can't wait to put mine on the tree next Christmas! We met Bob "Crocodile" Lile at his art gallery. He showed us how he makes beautiful jewelry from the paint chips off the cars at Cadillac Ranch.

Penny was excited to discover bars of soap shaped like the Route 66 shield at Texas Ivy. She explained that they were made by friends of hers right here in Texas! They came in assorted colors and scents and Mommy let us each pick one.

↑ This arch made of ivy was so cool I couldn't wait to walk through it!

We left the historic district and stopped at The Big Texan, where you can get a 72 ounce steak for free if you are able to eat it all! Daddy said he didn't think all of us combined could eat that much in the time allowed! It was fun watching other people try, though!

Penny stopped at the "Bug Ranch" in Conway so we could paint our names on what is left of the "bugs" that are planted in the ground. I still haven't figured out why they plant their cars in Texas, but it's nice to know we could paint on them without getting into trouble!

As we approached Groom, we all laughed as we saw the Britten leaning tower. It had fooled us on our last trip; we thought it was a water tower, but learned it had been built to advertise a business.

The Alanreed Travel Center was a fun stop! It's filled with everything you can think of: snacks, gifts, ice cream, and even a post office! I mailed a post card to my friend, Molly Mole! You have to go inside to discover the legend of Snake Oil Willy! I was a little scared at first, but it didn't have anything to do with real snakes.

The restored "66 Service Station" looked different than most we'd seen. It was in a very lonely section of Alanreed. Down the road a ways I saw a cool sign. I had to ask Daddy what Burma Shave was! He explained that it was a shaving cream company famous for its roadside jingles on signs just like that one.

  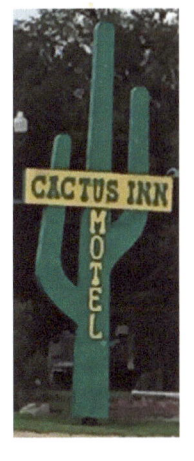

In McLean we visited the Devil's Rope Museum. I was so amazed by the barbed wire sculptures on our last trip, I didn't see the rest of the museum. After leaving the museum, Penny drove through town so Daddy could see the restored gas station that reminded him of his father's gas station. I spotted this cool motel sign along the way!

When we got to Shamrock we stopped at one of my favorite buildings on the route: the U-Drop Inn and Conoco Tower Station. It was once a gas station and restaurant, but now it's a visitor's center, museum and gift shop. Even though it's not a restaurant, the diner side is restored to look like it did a

long time ago. We all laughed at Billy when he tried to talk to the mannequin "waitress" behind the counter. The gift shop had a corner for kids to watch my favorite movie: CARS! After we left Penny showed us some of her other favorite places in Shamrock: A Magnolia Station and the Water Tower Plaza.

OKLAHOMA

And before we knew it, we were in Oklahoma and rolling into Texola.

As she pulled into the Tumbleweed Grill/Waterhole #2, Penny said, "This is the only diner I know of that's also an art gallery." We met the artist and admired her original artwork that lined the walls of the diner, while enjoying our milkshakes. After Penny chose another tee-shirt from the gift shop we said good-bye to another new friend on Route 66!

The National Route 66 Museum is located in Elk City at the Old Town Museum Complex. The buildings look like a small Old West town. This Kachina greeted us on our way inside. We learned the words "Yah-Ta-Hey" on the sign are a Navajo welcome greeting. As we walked through displays of each of the eight Route 66 states, we listened to recordings of people who shared their experiences living or working on Route 66. I had fun sitting in the driver's seat of a pink 1955 Cadillac and stepped on the gas pedal to start a video that showed what driving down Route 66 used to be like.

This sign for the Cotton Boll Motel in Canute still stands, even though the motel is no longer open.

I played miniature golf for the first time at McLain Rogers Park in Clinton!

40

We explored the Oklahoma Route 66 Museum. We were able to see how Route 66 changed through each decade and the different reasons people traveled Route 66. I'm glad we get to travel it for a road trip vacation and not because we have to leave Oklahoma because of dust storms, like they did during the Dust Bowl days! Back outside, my little brothers thought they could have a treat inside the "Valentine" diner that sits beside the museum, but I remembered from our last trip that it was part of the museum display.

Our last stop in Clinton was at the Mohawk Lodge Indian Store. We learned it's the oldest Indian store in Oklahoma and has been in business even before Oklahoma was a state! After seeing authentic Indian beaded items, Mommy helped me pick out beads so we could make a necklace when we get back home.

Lucille's Roadhouse in Weatherford is a diner designed to look like the original Lucille's gas station in Hydro. Lucille Hamons lived in and ran the

business for 59 years and was known as the "Mother of the Mother Road" because she took care of travelers who needed help when their cars broke down or they didn't have any food.

The Indian Trading Post Art Gallery in Calumet had Native American flutes for kids and I was allowed to get one as long as I promised not to play it in the van. It's almost like the one Mommy bought on our last trip at the Cherokee Trading Post across the road.

In Oklahoma City, Penny drove over Lake Overholser Bridge before stopping at Ann's Chicken Fry House. Penny said we had to try the chicken fried steak; it sure was yummy! So were the fried peaches! Brother Bobby was the first to spot the huge milk bottle standing on top of the triangle-shaped building.

This 18' tall bronze sculpture is of a Miniconjou chief who fought in the Battle of Little Big Horn. It is named "Touch the Clouds" and is at the entrance to the University of Central Oklahoma in Edmond.

Our next stop was at POPS in Arcadia. It has a 66-foot tall pop bottle sculpture in front of the building, and a diner and gift shop inside. The windows have bottles of pop in every color you could think of! We were each allowed to pick one. I picked blue, my favorite color.

 The main level of the Round Barn of Arcadia is part gift shop, part museum and the upper level is used for special events. Mommy bought a recipe card holder that looked like the barn. It was made from some of the original boards that were taken off the barn when it was restored. We went upstairs to see the wooden ceiling. It is amazing; I wonder how they made the boards curve like that!

Our last stop in Arcadia was at John Hargrove's "routeopia." He has replicas of many of the famous things from across the route, both inside and outside the building. He let us sit in the car that goes through the wall, just like he did the last time we were here!

Penny eased the van into the parking lot of Seaba Station Motorcycle Museum in Warwick. This was the stop Big Brother Sam had been waiting for since we left home. He couldn't believe how many different kinds of motorcycles were inside and he wanted them all!

This sculpture welcomed us to Chandler.

We had a lot of fun at the Route 66 Interpretive Center!

As Penny parked in front of McJerry's Route 66 Gallery she told Daddy to make sure he took the EZ Guide in with us. Inside, Penny introduced us to the artist, Jerry McClanahan, who's also the author of the EZ Guide! He autographed it for us. Daddy and Mommy bought one of his signed paintings, too! Mommy said every time we walk past the spot where it hangs on the wall at home, we would remember this special moment!

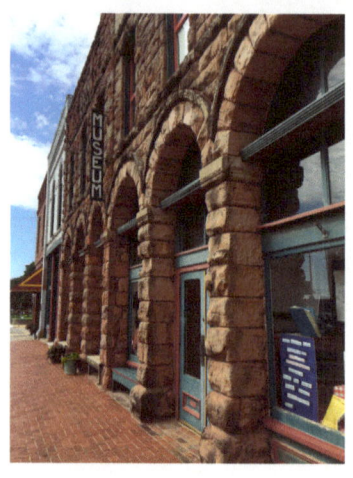

We were allowed to sit at a school desk used by pioneer children at the Lincoln County Museum of Pioneer History.

I liked the "thumpity thump" sound the tires made on the brick road in Davenport as we went down the street to look at the murals.

The Rock Café in Stroud was another great stop. On our way there, we saw a mural of the former Stroud train depot on the side of a building.

Outside the Heart of Route 66 Auto Museum in Sapulpa is a 66-foot-tall gas pump- the world's tallest!

On to Tulsa

In Tulsa, we stopped at the Cyrus Avery Centennial Plaza. Cyrus Avery is known as the "Father of Route 66" because of the role he played in developing Route 66. The bronze sculptures are called "East meets West" and show the Avery family in their car meeting up with an oil cart. Afterwards, we stopped at Ollie's Station Restaurant and watched the trains moving throughout the restaurant as we ate. My little brothers didn't want to leave!

Even though it's not a swimming park anymore, you CAN walk right into the mouth of the Blue Whale in Catoosa! And of course, Penny bought another tee shirt in the gift shop!

At the Will Rogers Memorial Museum in Claremore, we learned about the man who was known as "Oklahoma's favorite son." He was a famous actor, cowboy and newspaper columnist who was born in 1879. We were even able to watch some of his old movie clips in the museum's theater!

When Penny made the turn off of Route 66 to go to Ed Galloway's Totem Pole Park in Foyil, we discovered another diner named after ME! We had a great time at the park! My favorite part was seeing the 90-foot-tall world's largest concrete totem pole. We discovered the gift shop building is also decorated with totem poles and has a display of handmade fiddles inside.

After dinner at the Main Street Diner in Chelsea, we settled in for the night at the Chelsea Motor Inn. The next morning we walked UNDER Route 66 to see the mural and sign our names on the signature wall!

Afton Station Packard Museum was the stop Daddy had been waiting for since we left home. It has so many cool old cars, he couldn't wait to see it again! I liked the direction signs on the outside of the building.

We were treated to a tour of the Coleman Theater in Miami and even got to hear the original "Mighty Wurlitzer" pipe organ play!

After a yummy lunch at Waylan's Ku Ku Burger we stopped in Commerce for ice cream and Route 66 shield cookies at the Dairy King.

At the Oklahoma - Kansas state line, I asked Penny if she could stop so I could get a picture of the horse across the street. She turned the van around and we discovered the horse was a statue and part of an "Oklahoma Welcome" for those traveling west.

KANSAS

There are only about 13 miles of Route 66 that go through Kansas. Penny told us it was the only Route 66 state to be completely bypassed when the interstate came through. But there is still much to see and do!

Our first stop was in Baxter Springs. A sign on the Visitors Center building said it is a restored Phillips 66 station that was built in 1930 and was still used as a gas station until the 1970s. We learned that Baxter Springs was named after both the mineral springs that once ran through it and John Baxter, its first settler.

Here's a replica of John Baxter's Cabin and Trading Post.

Penny teased that we soon might not fit in her van with all the goodies we'd been eating! She suggested taking a walk through town. I was happy because I was able to take pictures of all of the cool signs. As we passed by the closed Ritz theater, Penny said she'd heard it was reopening soon.

The Crowell Bank was the first bank in Baxter Springs and was once robbed by the outlaw, Jesse James! The building has been used for several different businesses since the bank closed in 1887.

When Penny pulled into the parking lot of the Monarch Pharmacy, I wondered if she was sick. But when we went inside, we were surprised to find an old-fashioned soda fountain inside the drug store! Mommy said all drug stores used to have soda fountains like this. It's a good thing we took that walk!

Penny drove the van through the countryside and we went over the Marsh Rainbow Bridge, the last one of its kind on Route 66. I was proud of myself because I remembered it was called "rainbow bridge" because of its shape.

We sat on the covered patio to enjoy our yummy, freshly-made sandwiches at Nelson's Old Riverton store. As we ate, we watched the rain gently falling, watering the beautiful flowers that surrounded us. Of course, Penny checked out the tee shirts in the gift shop before we left!

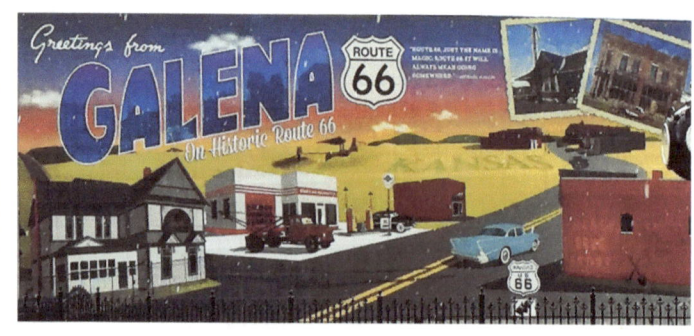

An old railroad depot is home to the Galena Mining and Historical Museum. I went with Mommy to check out the room with the old dolls, while Daddy and my brothers went to examine the mineral samples and see the model of a 1913 mine. After I saw all the dolls I went with Daddy to see the old vehicles.

Penny said her favorite thing at the museum was looking at old photographs and postcards of the town from a long time ago. She pointed out a postcard from the 1930s of the Front Street Garage, which was built in 1896. Since it was right around the corner, it was our next stop.

When we arrived, we discovered the owner, Ed, was working on restoring the building and it was not yet open for business. He told us the building provided some of the inspiration for the town, Radiator Springs, in my favorite movie, CARS!

Cars on the Route was our last stop in Kansas. We discovered a diner and gift shop inside. We learned that an old tow truck beside the building provided the inspiration for Mater, one of the characters in the CARS movie!

As she drove over the Galena viaduct, towards Missouri, Penny told us we were driving over original Route 66 roadbed!

When we crossed the state line from Kansas we were in Joplin, Missouri. We were sad to see that Carousel Park and all the rides were gone. But Penny quickly cheered us up by introducing us to Schifferdecker Park. We had a blast swimming and exploring the museums! Afterwards, as Penny drove through Joplin, I spotted this mural. We ended the day with a pizza from Woody's!

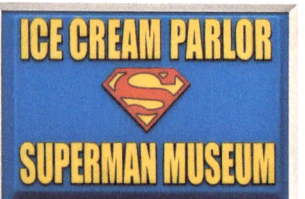

SuperTam on 66 in Carterville is not only an ice cream parlor, but a Superman museum, too! My brothers excitedly went from case to case looking at each of the displays, while I enjoyed my ice cream. On our way back to the van we skipped down the walkway stones that were shaped like each of the Route 66 states.

We strolled through the Carthage town square. The building that looks like a castle is the Jasper County Courthouse. It has a mini-museum inside and a really cool elevator with an elevator operator!

I heard Mommy and Daddy whispering to Penny so I knew another surprise was coming! Penny stopped the van at the Boots Court and announced we were staying overnight. All the rooms have old radios in them, just like they did in 1949! Brother Billy kept staring at the one in our room, wondering when a picture would appear! Daddy showed us how it worked, and Mommy told us this is what people did for entertainment before televisions were invented. Penny said we didn't need a television because we were going to the Carthage Drive-In! I was so excited to finally be going to a drive-in movie! I sat outside on a blanket with the older kids, eating popcorn, waiting for the movie to begin, but the next thing I remember was waking up inside my room at the Boots Court!

We took a side trip to Red Oak II, a small village created by the artist, Lowell Davis. We passed by many of his sculptures in the Carthage area. Mommy called them "whimsical!"

As Penny drove through the countryside, we passed this colorful building in Avilla and what was once a row of businesses in Spencer, before crossing the bridge.

51

At Gary's Gay Parita Sinclair Station in Paris Springs, we met Gary's daughter, who was now greeting Route 66 travelers, just like her father used to. She showed us the memorial garden she created for her parents and asked us to sign the memorial fence. On our last trip Gary said we would be "friends for life" and he will always be in our hearts.

Whitehall Mercantile in Halltown is the oldest building in town and was originally a general store.

I was fooled by the Modern Cabins sign at Graystone Heights Motor Courts! I thought we were going to be staying there but discovered the cabins have been part of R & S Florals since 1963. We were able to see what it would have been like to stay in one of the cabins in 1939 and learned that running water was a luxury back then!

As Penny drove towards Springfield, she told us that highway officials met in Springfield, Missouri in 1926 and named the route U.S. 66, so now Springfield is known as the birthplace of Route 66!

52

There were many interesting things to see and do in Springfield.

After touring Springfield, we checked in to the Best Western Route 66 Rail Haven. We met Route 66 travelers from around the world at the pool and even made new friends from Belgium and Germany!

We went on a safari in Strafford! The animals came right up to the bus looking for food at the Wild Animal Safari Drive-thru Animal Park! Everyone laughed when a camel slobbered on me!

53

Lebanon's library holds many surprises! Not only is it a great library, it has a Route 66 Museum and Kinderhook Treasures gift shop inside, too! We enjoyed seeing the miniature models of the Riviera Roadhouse, Gay Parita's, and Diamond Restaurant created by the Netherlands artist, Willem Bor, inside the museum. Afterwards, we checked in to the Munger Moss Motel, where we met many other Route 66 travelers in the gazebo. As the neon sign flashed, we enjoyed our sandwiches from The Vintage Cowgirl@Wrink's Market, while we made new friends from all over the world.

As Penny drove through the beautiful Missouri countryside she passed through Hazelgreen, Waynesville, St. Robert and Devil's Elbow before stopping at Larry Baggett's Trail of Tears Memorial. Penny told us she was happy to see that the crumbling stonework was repaired so the monument will continue to welcome visitors and honor the Native Americans who passed through this area.

In Rolla we stopped at the Totem Pole Trading Post, which claims to be Missouri's oldest business! They even have a totem pole inside!

We had fun searching for treasures at The Mule Trading Post!

 We felt really tiny next to the huge rocker at the Fanning Outpost! It was in the Guinness Book of World Records for being the largest rocking chair in the world until 2016, when someone built a larger rocker!

We visited Bob's Gasoline Alley in Cuba. I've never seen so many signs in one place!

Cuba is known as Mural City because of the amazing murals throughout town. I thought some of the people on the sides of the buildings were real!

We had delicious barbecue ribs at Missouri Hicks and when we came out, the sign for the Wagon Wheel Motel was lit up!

We stopped for another great treat at the Circle Inn Malt Shop in Bourbon!

I watched Daddy using a chain saw before, but I never knew people could make such beautiful artwork with them until we stopped at Creative Chainsaw Carvings!

After we learned that Jesse James used the Meramec Caverns as a hideout, we wanted to know more about him. At the Jesse James Museum, not only did we learn more about the outlaw and the James Gang, we saw models of an old bank and post office and many antiques from the 1800s. You'll have to take the tour to discover the mystery surrounding what happened to Jesse James!

Even though Penny said we might not be able to all fit back in the van if we ate more ice cream, she decided we just couldn't pass up a Ted Drewes "concrete" in St. Louis.

As we passed the St. Louis arch we said good-bye to Missouri.

We all clapped and cheered as we entered Illinois- the last state of our eastward Route 66 journey!

When we saw the Hen House in Mitchell, Little Sister Sally asked if we could stop and see the chickens! Then Jenny got in trouble for making fun of her.

As she drove through Edwardsville, Penny told us to look for Information Centers along the route in Illinois. This one displayed Route 66 through Illinois. It also had a button to push for us to listen to the song, "Get Your Kicks on Route 66!" We sang along and danced to the music!

We got excited when we saw the "Hare It Is" sign come into view in Staunton! We couldn't wait to visit with the bunnies at Henry's Rabbit Ranch! Mr. Henry even let us pet one, warning us to be gentle!

In Mount Olive we stopped at the Soulsby Shell Station, designed and built by Henry Soulsby in 1926 to fit in with the houses in the neighborhood. It has been restored to how it would have looked in the 1940s. Afterwards, Penny drove through the Union Miners Cemetery to see the Mother Jones Monument.

In Litchfield we enjoyed our meals at the Ariston Café then toured the Litchfield Museum & Route 66 Welcome Center. There was a lot to see! My favorite section was the Bob Waldmire display.

Photographed by Anne M. Slanina.
Used with permission of the Litchfield Museum.

Mommy went into Jubelt's and bought pastries for us that were DE-LICIOUS!!

As Penny drove through Carlinville she pointed out what she called "Sears homes." She explained that they were built from kits ordered from a Sears catalog and there are over 100 of them still standing in this neighborhood! I thought she was joking, but Mommy added that at one time big catalogs used to come in the mail and people ordered anything you could think of from them. She said she'd heard there was a special catalog just for houses!

We also saw the Carlinville historic jail and the Million Dollar Court House. It's called that because it cost over a MILLION dollars to build in 1870!!

Doc's Soda Fountain and a pharmacy museum are inside what was once Deck's Drug Store, which opened in 1884. At one time most drug stores had a soda fountain counter. The original, old-fashioned soda fountain is still in use here, serving yummy treats and lunches! We had fun checking out the display of items from the original pharmacy.

Penny drove through Virden and down the brick road in Auburn before stopping in Springfield. I liked the "thumpity-thump" sound the tires made on the brick road.

We spent several days in Springfield, staying at the Route 66 Motel & Conference Center, and exploring historic sites. After checking in and cooling off in the pool, we walked down the street to the Cozy Dog Drive In. While waiting for the best corn dogs we've ever eaten, we explored the displays throughout the restaurant and learned about how the parents of the famous Route 66 artist, Bob Waldmire, invented the corn dog and started the restaurant. We learned the corn dogs had originally been called "crusty curs."

We visited Lincoln's Tomb, President Lincoln's home, and the State Capitol buildings. We discovered another Muffler Man at Lauterbach Tire & Auto Service!

We were disappointed to see that Shea's Gas Station Museum was closed and all the memorabilia was gone. Penny said there had been an auction and everything had been sold,  including Mahan's service station, which was now on display outside of Fulgenzi's Pizza and Pasta shop. It was a double treat to see it AND get some pizza!

 Penny told us this marker in Broadwell was placed to honor the memory of Ernie Edwards, who owned The Pig Hip Restaurant. This sign marks the spot where the Pig Hip Restaurant once stood.

The Railsplitter Covered Wagon is "The World's Largest Covered Wagon" according to the Guinness Book of World Records. It is 24 feet tall!

These would be perfect for spotting storms from the rooftop phone booth!

Lincoln's City Hall has a phone booth on the roof! Penny said that it was put there in the 1960s for someone to spot severe weather and send a warning to an office in city hall.

Our last stop in Lincoln was at The Mill Museum and Gift Shop. Can you guess what Penny bought in the gift shop?

Atlanta was a fun stop! We could see the smiling water tower as we came into town. First, we stopped to see "Tall Paul," the Muffler Man that's holding a hot dog. Then we had delicious pie at the Palms Grill Café. Afterwards, we walked down the street to explore the 1908 Clock Tower, Library & Museum.

To end the day, Penny stopped at the Dixie Family Restaurant inside the Dixie Truckers Home in McClean. While having our dinner we learned it is the oldest truck stop in America!

Mommy couldn't wait to get some delicious maple "sirup" at Funks Grove, and neither could I! Penny couldn't wait to get another tee-shirt!

Ryburn Place at Sprague's Super Service is a unique gift shop and information center in Normal. It is one of only five two-story service stations along the route and was built in 1931. When it was built, it was a gas station, garage, café and had apartments upstairs!

Penny drove through Lexington's Memory Lane on our way to Pontiac. As we entered the town, Penny pointed out the beautiful town square.

We stopped at The Old City Hall Shoppes. Inside the complex, we toured the Illinois Route 66 Hall of Fame and Museum, where we saw Bob Waldmire's 1972 VW Microbus that he used to tour the Route in! Waldmire also used an old school bus that he converted into a home-on-wheels to travel in. It's on display behind the museum and we were able to go inside! The building also includes a World War II Museum and a Walldogs Museum. We learned the Walldogs are a worldwide group of artists who were responsible for painting many of the amazing murals found throughout Pontiac. Before leaving the former city hall and fire station building, we shopped in Home Again Gift & Souvenirs. It was filled with many unique items, some which were created by Joyce, the artist and owner of the shop. Yes, Penny bought ANOTHER tee-shirt!

We also explored the Pontiac-Oakland Automobile Museum, where we learned the town was named after Chief Pontiac, who was an Ottawa Indian admired by some of the early settlers to the area. The museum displays the history of the Oakland and Pontiac automobiles.

We'd never heard of Oakland cars before, but I thought they looked pretty cool! This one is a 1929 Oakland Roadster.

The volunteer at The Village of Odell's Welcome Center told us the building was originally built in 1932 as a Standard Oil gas station. Mommy found some post cards for her collection.

The Ambler-Becker Texaco Gas Station in Dwight is now a visitors' center. It opened in 1933 and served travelers for 66 years before closing in 1999. We were allowed to sit on the fire truck inside!

It was hot and we thought we were stopping for cold drinks, but we were fooled by the signs for refreshments on this building in Gardner! Inside, we found Perkins Wood and Glass, a stained-glass shop. Not only did we see how stained-glass windows are created, we enjoyed the Route 66 memorabilia throughout the building.

The Route 66 Streetcar Diner that sits beside the Gardner jail was originally a horse-drawn streetcar, and later converted to a diner. It doesn't serve food anymore, but it has been restored and we were allowed to look inside.

This small "zoo" welcomed us to Braidwood! Penny told us the animals were created by the artist, Jack Barker, from recycled materials.

The Polk-A-Dot Drive-In was a perfect stop for refreshments!

This dinosaur on top of a building in Wilmington made us giggle!

We were happy to see the Gemini Giant, another one of our favorite Muffler Men, still standing in Wilmington next to the Launching Pad Drive In. Penny bought another tee-shirt inside the gift shop!

After seeing the mural painted on the side of the building,  Penny said we HAD to stop at Two Hounds antique shop. Daddy took us for a walk down the street so Mommy and Penny could shop. Daddy said all of us kids around antiques makes him nervous!

Our next stop was Joliet, which meant we had to cross the Des Plaines River over the Ruby Street Bridge. Just as we approached, the drawbridge began to raise! It was so cool to watch, we didn't mind that we had to wait awhile to cross the bridge!

There were a lot of fun things to see in Joliet! Penny said those are the Blues Brothers dancing on top the Rich & Creamy ice cream stand! This towing company display made us laugh!

We enjoyed visiting the Joliet Area Historical Museum and Route 66 Visitors Center. Afterwards we walked around town. Here are a few of my favorite things: The Rialto Square Theater and Joliet Route 66 Diner.

This big chicken welcomed us to White Fence Farm in Romeoville, where we stopped for dinner. Daddy said it was "an experience," as he licked his fingers! We all had fun putting our faces in this sign.

On the way to Chicago, Penny drove through Berwyn and Cicero. Maybe on our next trip we'll try the hot dogs at Henry's.

 Arriving in Chicago was exciting — we had reached the end of our Route 66 adventure. Penny said that the official beginning of Route 66 is near Lou Mitchell's, so we started our morning there with a delicious breakfast.

Afterwards, we spent the day exploring the city.

Art Institute

A Cool Globe Sculpture outside Willis Tower

Harold Washington Library Center

Before Penny took us to the airport, Daddy said we needed to take one more family photo to mark the end our Route 66 adventure. We all agreed that this one had to include Cousin Penny, who is now an official member of our family!

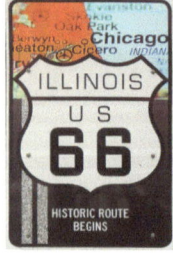 Chicago also has an End of the Route sign for people like us, who are traveling west to east. It was the last photo I took before we left Chicago.

On our flight home we talked about all the things that stayed the same from our first adventure and all the things that changed. We decided that no matter how many times you visit Route 66, it will be a new adventure! We already miss Penny and we've already started planning our next trip!

Dedications

This book is dedicated to the Route 66 business owners, past and present, who built and continue to keep the spirit of the Mother Road alive. It is also dedicated to those who work tirelessly to preserve the historic value of the Route, whether it be through their preservation efforts, art work, blogs, books, music, or purchases. With a special "thank you" to all of those who have befriended me along the Route, helping me to have the time of my life! And an extra-special "thank you" to my dear friend, Penny Black, who agreed to having her likeness used as the tour guide, Cousin Penny, in this book. She is always willing to drop everything and become an unofficial tour guide to Route 66 "roadies."

Finally, an extra-special "THANK YOU" goes out to David P. Keppel, whose tireless work on the design and layout of this book make it possible to see print!

A Note to Travelers

Please note that businesses along Route 66, as all over the country, change constantly. Route 66 information was accurate at the time of publication. Please enjoy your trip along the Mother Road and always watch out for your own safety! You can use the inside covers to collect signatures for your own trips along The Mother Road.

Resources

Klein, Ed. Owner of the Front Street Garage, Galena, KS. Email correspondence March 16, 2018.

Hinckley, Jim. Ghost Towns of Route 66. (2011). Voyageur Press.

Hinckley, Jim. (2012). The Route 66 Encyclopedia. Voyageur Press.

Illinoisroute66.org

McClanahan, Jerry. (2013). EZ66 Guide for Travelers: Third edition. National Historic Route 66 Federation.

Ross, Jim & McClanahan, Jerry. (2005). Here It Is! The Route 66 Map Series. Ghost Town Press.

Snyder, Tom. (2000). Route 66: Traveler's Guide and Roadside Companion. St. Martin's Griffin.

Wallis, Michael. (2006). The Art of Cars. Disney Enterprises, Inc./Pixar Animation Studios.

Wallis, Michael. (2001). Route 66: The Mother Road 75th Anniversary Edition. St. Martin's Griffin.

Wickline, David. (2006). Images of 66: An Interactive Photographic Journey Along the Length of the Mother Road. Roadhouse 66, LLC.

Wickline, David. (2008). Images of 66 Volume 2: Digging Deeper Along the Length of Historic Route 66. Roadhouse 66, LLC.

www.Route66News.com

Copyright ©2018 by Anne Maro Slanina, Ph.D.

Library of Congress Control Number: 2018905910
ISBN Print Edition: 978-0-9914094-3-3
ISBN E-Book Edition: 978-0-9914094-4-0

To order additional copies of the book, contact:
Annie Mouse Books
P.O. Box 142
Harrisville, PA 16038

www.anniemousebooks.com
anniemousebooks@gmail.com

All rights reserved. No part of this publication may be reproduced or transmitted in any form or by any means, electronic or mechanical, including photocopy, recording, or any information storage system, without permission in writing from the publisher.

The Blues Brothers is a registered trademark owned by Applied Action Research Corp and Judith Belushi. Cadillac Ranch © 1974 ANT FARM. Cadillac is a registered trademark of General Motors Corporation. Cars (the movie) is a 2006 Disney/Pixar production. Get Your Kicks on Route 66" was written by Bobby Troup (1946) and originally recorded by Nat King Cole. Jimmy Stewart Museum (The) is dedicated to the life and career of actor James Stewart, located on the third floor of the Indiana, Pennsylvania Public Library on the corner of 9th and Philadelphia streets. Standin' on a corner in Winslow, Arizona," is from the song, Take it Easy, written by Jackson Browne and Glenn Frey (1972) and recorded by The Eagles. It's a Wonderful Life is a 1946 Frank Capra Liberty Films production. Superman is a registered trademark of D.C. Comics and Warner Brothers. Ted Drewes Frozen Custard is a registered trademark and brand of Ted Drewes, Inc. It's signature treat is the "concrete." The Book of Modern Homes. (1940). Chicago: Sears, Roebuck and Company. (Now in the public domain.) Volkswagen is a registered trademark of Volkswagen AG and Volkswagen of America.

Quotes attributed to the Mouse Family's "guide book" or "travel guide" and "Penny" are not actual quotes, but represent information compiled from the author's travels, the owners of businesses along the route and from a variety of books and web sites listed as "Resources."

All names and likenesses of actual people are used with permission.

Unless otherwise noted, photographs of landmarks and businesses were taken by the author.

This book was printed in the United States of America.

www.ingramcontent.com/pod-product-compliance
Lightning Source LLC
Chambersburg PA
CBHW041440010526
44118CB00002B/133